JN299290

少女時代

美智子

橋をかける

文藝春秋

この本は、1998年に㈱すえもりブックスから刊行されたものを文藝春秋が引き継ぎ、内容、判型、装丁などそのままに復刊したものです。

橋をかける　子供時代の読書の思い出

2012年 4月15日　第1刷発行
2023年 9月25日　第9刷発行

著者　　美智子
発行者　　花田朋子
発行所　　株式会社文藝春秋
〒102-8008　東京都千代田区紀尾井町 3-23
電話　03-3265-1211（代表）
印刷・製本　精興社

ISBN 978-4-16-375310-2
Printed in Japan

定価はカバーに表示してあります。万一、落丁・乱丁の場合は送料当方負担でお取替えいたします。小社製作部宛、お送り下さい。
本書の無断複写は著作権法上での例外を除き禁じられています。また、私的使用以外のいかなる電子的複製行為も一切認められておりません。

本書は、一九九八年九月二十日から二十四日までインドのニューデリー、アショカ・ホテルで開催された国際児童図書評議会―International Board on Books for Young People（IBBY）―第二十六回世界大会において、本会議初日の二十一日朝、ビデオテープによって上映された皇后様の基調講演を収録したものです。
編集に当たり、ニューデリーの講演では時間の都合上削られた箇所も元に戻し、初稿を元に定本といたしました。

橋をかける　もくじ

子供時代の読書の思い出 ……………………………………… 1

皇后様とIBBYの人たち ……………… 島　多代 29

注 ………………………………………………………………… 35

装丁・絵　安野光雅

第二十六回IBBYニューデリー大会（一九九八年）基調講演

子供の本を通しての平和
——子供時代の読書の思い出——

美智子

ジャファ夫人、デアルデン夫人、IBBYの皆様

第二十六回国際児童図書評議会（IBBY）ニューデリー大会の開催に当たり、思いがけず基調講演者としてお招きを受けました。残念なことに、直接会議に参加することが出来ず、このような形でお話をさせて頂くことになりましたが、遠く日本より、この度のニューデリー大会の開催をお祝いし、御招待に対し厚くお礼を申し上げます。

大会の行われている印度の国に、私は沢山の懐かしい思い出を持っています。一九六〇年、当時皇太子でいらした天皇陛下と共に印度を訪れた時、私は二十六歳で、生後九ヶ月になる一児の若い母であり、その十三年前、長い希望の年月を経て独立を果たした印度は、プラサド大統領、ラダクリシュナン副大統領、ネルー首相の時代でした。この方々のお話──自由と民主主義、平和への思い──を、心深く伺った日々、又、人々の歓迎に包まれて、カルカッタ、ニューデリー、ボンベイ、アグラ、ブダガヤ、パトナを旅した日々のことを、今懐かしく思い出しつつ、印度国際児童図書評議会によりとり行われる今大会の御成功を、心からお祈りいたします。

大会のテーマである「子供の本を通しての平和」につき、私にどのようなお話が出来るでしょうか。今から三年前、一九九五年三月に、IBBYの印度支部会長、ジャファ夫人のお手紙を受けとったその日から、私は何回となく、この事を自分に問いかけて来ました。

私は、多くの方々と同じく、今日まで本から多くの恩恵を受けてまいりました。子供の頃は遊びの一環として子供の本を楽しみ、成人してからは大人の本を、そして数は多くはないのですが、ひき続き子供の本を楽しんでいます。結婚後三人の子供に恵まれ、かつて愛読した児童文学を、再び子供と共に読み返す喜びを与えられると共に、新しい時代の児童文学を知る喜びも与えられたことは、誠に幸運なことでした。

もし子供を持たなかったなら、私は赤ずきんやアルプスのハイジ、モーグリ少年の住んだジャングルについては知っていても、森の中で動物たちと隠れん坊をするエッツの男の子とも、レオ・レオーニの「あおくん」や「きいろちゃん」とも巡り会うことは出来なかったかもしれないし、バートンの「ちいさいおうち」の歴史を知ること

もなかったかもしれません。トールキンやC・S・ルイス、ローズマリー・サトクリフ、フィリッパ・ピアス等の名も、すでに子供たちの母となってから目を通して知りました。しかし、先にも述べたように、私はあくまでごく限られた数の本しか目を通しておらず、研究者、専門家としての視点からお話をする力は持ちません。又、児童文学と平和という今回の主題に関しても、私は非常に間接的にしか、この二つを結びつけることが出来ないのではないかと案じています。

児童文学と平和とは、必ずしも直線的に結びついているものではないでしょう。又、云うまでもなく、一冊、又は数冊の本が、平和への扉を開ける鍵であるというようなことも、あり得ません。今日、この席で、もし私に出来ることが何かあるとすれば、それは自分の子供時代の読書経験をふり返り、自分の中に、その後の自分の考え方、感じ方の「芽」になるようなものを残したと思われる何冊かの本を思い出し、それにつきお話をしてみることではないかと思います。そして、わずかであれ、それを今大会の主題である、「平和」という脈絡の中に置いて考えてみることができればと願っています。

生まれて以来、人は自分と周囲との間に、一つ一つ橋をかけ、人とも、物ともつながりを深め、それを自分の世界として生きています。この橋がかからなかったり、かけても橋としての機能を果たさなかったり、時として橋をかける意志を失った時、人は孤立し、平和を失います。この橋は外に向かうだけでなく、内にも向かい、自分と自分自身との間にも絶えずかけ続けられ、本当の自分を発見し、自己の確立をうながしていくように思います。

私の子供の時代は、戦争による疎開生活をはさみながらも、年長者の手に護られた、比較的平穏なものであったと思います。そのような中でも、度重なる生活環境の変化は、子供には負担であり、私は時に周囲との関係に不安を覚えたり、なかなか折り合いのつかない自分自身との関係に、疲れてしまったりしていたことを覚えています。

そのような時、何冊かの本が身近にあったことが、どんなに自分を楽しませ、励まし、個々の問題を解かないまでも、自分を歩き続けさせてくれたか。私の限られた経験が、果たして何かのお役に立つものかと心配ですが、思い出すままにお話をしてみたいと思います。

まだ小さな子供であった時に、一匹のでんでん虫の話を聞かせてもらったことがあります。不確かな記憶ですので、今、恐らくはそのお話の元はこれではないかと思われる、新美南吉の「でんでん虫のかなしみ」にそってお話いたします。そのでんでん虫は、ある日突然、自分の背中の殻に、悲しみが一杯つまっていることに気付き、友達を訪ね(たず)、もう生きていけないのではないか、と自分の背負っている不幸を話します。友達のでんでん虫は、それはあなただけではない、私の背中の殻にも、悲しみは一杯つまっている、と答えます。小さなでんでん虫は、別の友達、又別の友達と訪ねて行き、同じことを話すのですが、どの友達からも返って来る答は同じでした。そして、でんでん虫はやっと、悲しみは誰でも持っているのだ、ということに気付きます。自分だけではないのだ。私は、私の悲しみをこらえていかなければならない。この話は、このでんでん虫が、もうなげくのをやめたところで終っています。

あの頃、私は幾つくらいだったのでしょう。母や、母の父である祖父、叔父や叔母たちが本を読んだりお話をしてくれたのは、私が小学校の二年くらいまででしたから、

四歳から七歳くらいまでの間であったと思います。その頃、私はまだ大きな悲しみというものを知りませんでした。だからでしょう。最後になげくのをやめた、と知った時、簡単にああよかった、と思いました。それだけのことで、特にこのことにつき、じっと思いをめぐらせたということでもなかったのです。

しかし、この話は、その後何度となく、思いがけない時に私の記憶に甦って来ました。殻一杯になる程の悲しみということと、ある日突然そのことに気付き、もう生きていけないと思ったでんでん虫の不安とが、私の記憶に刻みこまれていたのでしょう。少し大きくなると、はじめて聞いた時のように、「ああよかった」だけでは済まされなくなりました。生きていくということは、楽なことではないのだという、何とはない不安を感じることもありました。それでも、私は、この話が決して嫌いではありませんでした。

私が小学校に入る頃に戦争が始まりました。昭和十六年（一九四一年）のことです。四学年に進級する頃には戦況が悪くなり、生徒達はそれぞれに縁故を求め、又は学校

集団として、田舎に疎開していきました。私の家では父と兄が東京に残り、私は妹と弟と共に、母につれられて海辺に、山に、住居を移し、三度目の疎開先で終戦を迎えました。

度重なる移居と転校は子供には負担であり、異なる風土、習慣、方言の中での生活には、戸惑いを覚えることも少なくありませんでしたが、田舎での生活は、時に病気がちだった私をすっかり健康にし、私は蚕を飼ったり、草刈りをしたり、時にはゲンノショーコとカラマツ草を、それぞれ干して四キロずつ供出するという、宿題のノルマにも挑戦しました。八キロの干草は手には持ちきれず、母が背中に負わせてくれ、学校まで運びました。牛乳が手に入らなくなり、母は幼い弟のために山羊を飼い、その世話と乳しぼりを私にまかせてくれました。

教科書以外にほとんど読む本のなかったこの時代に、たまに父が東京から持ってきてくれる本は、どんなに嬉しかったか。冊数が少ないので、惜しみ惜しみ読みました。そのような中の一冊に、今、題を覚えていないのですが、子供のために書かれた日本の神話伝説の本がありました。日本の歴史の曙のようなこの時代を物語る神話や伝説

は、どちらも八世紀に記された二冊の本、古事記と日本書紀に記されていますから、恐らくはそうした本から、子供向けに再話されたものだったのでしょう。

父がどのような気持ちからその本を選んだのか、寡黙な父から、その時も、その後も聞いたことはありません。しかしこれは、今考えると、本当によい贈り物であったと思います。なぜなら、それから間もなく戦争が終わり、米軍の占領下に置かれた日本では、教育の方針が大巾に変わり、その後は歴史教育の中から、神話や伝説は全く削除されてしまったからです。

私は、自分が子供であったためか、民族の子供時代のようなこの太古の物語を、大変面白く読みました。今思うのですが、一国の神話や伝説は、正確な史実ではないかもしれませんが、不思議とその民族を象徴します。これに民話の世界を加えると、それぞれの国や地域の人々が、どのような自然観や生死観を持っていたか、何を尊び、何を恐れたか、どのような想像力を持っていたか等が、うっすらとですが感じられます。

父がくれた神話伝説の本は、私に、個々の家族以外にも、民族の共通の祖先がある

ことを教えたという意味で、私に一つの根っこのようなものを与えてくれました。本というものは、時に子供に安定の根を与え、時にどこにでも飛んでいける翼を与えてくれるもののようです。もっとも、この時の根っこは、かすかに自分の帰属を知ったという程のもので、それ以後、これが自己確立という大きな根に少しずつ育っていく上の、ほんの第一段階に過ぎないものではあったのですが。

又、これはずっと後になって認識したことなのですが、この本は、日本の物語の原型ともいうべきものを私に示してくれました。やがてはその広大な裾野に、児童文学が生まれる力強い原型です。そしてこの原型との子供時代の出会いは、その後私が異国を知ろうとする時に、何よりもまず、その国の物語を知りたいと思うきっかけを作ってくれました。私にとり、フィンランドは第一にカレワラ[11]の国であり、アイルランドはオシーン[12]やリヤ[13]の子供達の国、インドはラマヤナ[14]やジャータカ[15]の国、メキシコはポポル・ブフ[16]の国です。これだけがその国の全てでないことは勿論ですが、他国に親しみをもつ上で、これは大層楽しい入口ではないかと思っています。

二、三十年程前から、「国際化」「地球化」という言葉をよくきくようになりました。

しかしこうしたことは、ごく初歩的な形で、もう何十年——もしかしたら百年以上も前から——子供の世界では本を通じ、ゆるやかに始まっていたといえないでしょうか。一九九六年の「子供の本の日」のためにIBBYが作ったポスターには、世界の家々を象徴する沢山の屋根を見おろす上空に、ぽっかりと浮かんで、楽しげに本をよんでいる一人の少年が描かれていました。遠く離れた世界のあちこちの国で、子供達はもう何年も何年も前から、同じ物語を共有し、同じ物語の主人公に親しんで来たのです。

父のくれた古代の物語の中で、一つ忘れられない話がありました。年代の確定出来ない、六世紀以前の一人の皇子の物語です。倭建御子と呼ばれるこの皇子は、父天皇の命を受け、遠隔の反乱の地に赴いては、これを平定して凱旋するのですが、あたかもその皇子の力を恐れているかのように、天皇は新たな任務を命じ、皇子に平穏な休息を与えません。悲しい心を抱き、皇子は結局これが最後となる遠征に出かけます。途中、海が荒れ、皇子の船は航路を閉ざされます。この時、付き添っていた后、弟橘比売命は、自分が海に入り海神のいかりを鎮めるので、皇子

はその使命を遂行し覆奏してほしい、と云い入水し、皇子の船を目的地に向かわせます。この時、弟橘は、美しい別れの歌を歌います。

さねさし相武の小野に燃ゆる火の火中に立ちて問ひし君はも

このしばらく前、建と弟橘とは、広い枯れ野を通っていた時に、敵の謀に会って草に火を放たれ、燃えさかる火に追われて逃げまどい、九死に一生を得たのでした。弟橘の歌は、「あの時、燃えさかる火の中で、私の安否を気遣って下さった君よ」という、危急の折に皇子の示した、優しい庇護の気遣いに対する感謝の気持を歌ったものです。悲しい「いけにえ」の物語は、それまでも幾つかは知っていました。しかし、この物語の犠牲は、少し違っていました。弟橘の言動には、何と表現したらよいか、建と任務を分かち合うような、どこか意志的なものが感じられ、弟橘の歌は──私は今、それが子供向けに現代語に直されていたのか、原文のまま解説が付されていたのか思い出すことが出来ないのですが──あまりにも美しいものに思われました。「いけに

え」という酷い運命を、進んで自らに受け入れながら、恐らくはこれまでの人生で、最も愛と感謝に満たされた瞬間の思い出を歌っていることに、感銘という以上に、強い衝撃を受けました。はっきりとした言葉にならないまでも、愛と犠牲という二つのものが、私の中で最も近いものとして、むしろ一つのものとして感じられた、不思議な経験であったと思います。

この物語は、その美しさの故に私を深くひきつけましたが、同時に、説明のつかない不安感で威圧するものでもありました。

古代ではない現代に、海を静めるために、洪水を防ぐために、一人の人間の生命が求められるとは、まず考えられないことです。ですから、人身御供というそのことを、私が恐れるはずはありません。しかし、弟橘の物語には、何かもっと現代にも通じる象徴性があるように感じられ、そのことが私を息苦しくさせていました。今思うと、それは愛というものが、時として過酷な形をとるものなのかも知れないという、やはり先に述べた愛と犠牲の不可分性への、恐れであり、畏怖であったように思います。

まだ、子供であったため、その頃は、全てをぼんやりと感じただけなのですが、こ

12

うしたよく分からない息苦しさが、物語の中の水に沈むというイメージと共に押し寄せて来て、しばらくの間、私はこの物語にずい分悩まされたのを覚えています。

疎開中に父が持って来てくれた本の中で、あと三冊、私の思い出に残っている本があります。これは兄の持っていた本で、いつか読みたいと思っていたものを、父に頼んで借りてきてもらったものでした。三冊共「日本少国民文庫」というシリーズに含まれていました。「少国民文庫」は全部で十五、六冊あり、「人間はどれだけの事をして来たか」「人類の進歩につくした人々」「発明物語　科学手工」「スポーツと冒険物語」などという題で一冊ごとがまとめられています。父はこの時、その中の「日本名作選」一冊と、「世界名作選」二冊を選んで持って来てくれました。

この文庫が始めて刊行されたのは昭和十一年（一九三六年）、兄は五つで、私はまだ二つの頃です。その後戦争中の昭和十七年（一九四二年）に改訂版が出されており、母が兄のために買ったのは、兄の年令から見てもこれであったと思います。今私の手許にあるものは、今から十数年前に入手した、昭和十一年（一九三六年）版のうちの

数冊ですが、「名作選」の内容は記憶のものとほぼ一致しますので、戦前も戦中も、あまり変化はなかったものと思われます。

今こノ三冊の本のうち、「世界名作選」[20]二巻を開いてみると、キプリングのジャングル・ブックの中の「リッキ・ティキ・タヴィー物語」[21]や、ワイルドの「幸福の王子」[22]、カレル・チャペックの「郵便配達の話」[23]、トルストイの「人は何によって生きるか」[24]、シャルル・フィリップやチェーホフの手紙[25]、アン・モロー・リンドバーグの「日本紀行」[26]等が並んでいます。[27]ケストナーやマーク・トウェイン[28]、ロマン・ロラン[29]、ヘンリー・ヴァンダイク[30]、ラスキン等の名も見えます。必ずしも全部を熟読していない証拠に、内容の記憶がかすかなものもあります。

子供にも理解出来るような、いくつかの詩もありました。[31]カルル・ブッセ[32]、フランシス・ジャム[33]、ウイリアム・ブレイク[34]、ロバート・フロスト[35]…。私が、印度の詩人タゴール[36]の名を知ったのも、この本の中ででした。「花の学校」という詩が選ばれていました。後年、「新月」という詩集の中に、この詩を再び見出した時、どんなに嬉しかったことか。「花の学校」は、私をすぐに同じ詩人によ

14

る「あかんぼの道」や「審く人」、「チャンパの花」へと導いていきました。

ケストナーの「絶望」は、非常にかなしい詩でした。小さな男の子が、汗ばんだ手に一マルクを握って、パンとベーコンを買いに小走りに走っています。街のショー・ウィンドーの灯はだんだんと消え、方々の店の戸が締まり始めます。少年の両親は、一日の仕事の疲れの中で、子供の帰りを待っています。その子が家の前まで来て、壁に顔を向け、じっと立っているのを知らずに。心配になった母親が捜しに出て、子供を見つけます。いったいどこにいたの、と尋ねられ、子供は激しく泣き出します。「彼の苦しみは、母の愛より大きかった／二人はしょんぼりと家に入っていった」という言葉で終っています。

この「世界名作選」には、この「絶望」の他にも、ロシアのソログーブという作家の「身体検査」という悲しい物語が入っています。貧しい家の子供が、学校で盗みの疑いをかけられ、ポケットや靴下、服の中まで調べられている最中に、別の所から盗難品が出てきて疑いが晴れるという物語で、この日帰宅した子供から一部始終をきいた母親が、「何もいえないんだからね。大きくなったら、こんなことどころじゃない。

この世にはいろんな事があるからね」と歎く言葉がつけ加えられています。
思い出すと、戦争中にはとかく人々の志気を高めようと、勇ましい話が多かったように思うのですが、そうした中でこの文庫の編集者が、「絶望」やこの「身体検査」のような話を、何故ここに選んで載せたのか興味深いことです。
生きている限り、避けることの出来ない多くの悲しみに対し、ある時期から子供に備えさせなければいけない、という思いがあったのでしょうか。そしてお話の中のでんでん虫のように、悲しみは誰もが皆負っているのだということを、子供に知ってほしいという思いがあったのでしょうか。
私は、この文庫の編集企画をした山本有三につき、二、三の小説や戯曲による以外詳しくは知らないのですが、「日本名作選」及び「世界名作選」を編集するに当たっては、子供に喜びも悲しみも、深くこれを味わってほしいという、有三と、その協力者達の強い願いがあったのではないかと感じられてなりません。
本から得た「喜び」についても、ここで是非お話をさせて頂きたいと思います。た

16

しかに、世の中にさまざまな悲しみのあることを知ることは、時に私の心を重くし、暗く沈ませました。しかし子供は不思議なバランスのとり方をするもので、こうして少しずつ、本の中で世の中の悲しみにふれていったと同じ頃、私は同じく本の中に、大きな喜びも見出していっていたのです。この喜びは、心がいきいきと躍動し、生きていることへの感謝が湧き上がって来るような、快い感覚とでも表現したらよいでしょうか。

初めてこの意識を持ったのは、東京から来た父のカバンに入っていた小型の本の中に、一首の歌を見つけた時でした。それは春の到来を告げる美しい歌で、日本の五七五七七の定型で書かれていました。その一首をくり返し心の中で誦していると、古来から日本人が愛し、定型としたリズムの快さの中で、言葉がキラキラと光って喜んでいるように思われました。詩が人の心に与える喜びと高揚を、私はこの時初めて知ったのです。先に私は、本から与えられた「根っこ」のことをお話いたしましたが、今ここで述べた「喜び」は、これから先に触れる「想像力」と共に、私には自分の心を高みに飛ばす、強い「翼」のように感じられました。

「世界名作選」の編集者は、悲しく心の沈む「絶望」の詩と共に、こうした心の踊る喜びの歌を、その選に入れるのを忘れてはいませんでした。ロバート・フロストの「牧場」という詩は、私にそうした喜びを与えてくれた詩の一つでした。短い詩なので読んでみます。

「牧場」

牧場の泉を掃除しに行ってくるよ。
ちょっと落葉をかきのけるだけだ。
(でも水が澄むまで見てるかも知れない)
すぐ帰ってくるんだから―君も来たまへ

小牛をつかまへに行ってくるよ。
母牛のそばに立ってるんだがまだ赤ん坊で
母牛が舌でなめるとよろけるんだよ。
すぐ帰ってくるんだから―君も来たまへ

この詩のどこに、喜びの源があるのか、私に十分説明することは出来ません。勿論その詩の内容が、とても感じのよいものなのですが、この詩の用語の中にも、幾つかの秘密が隠れているようです。どれも快い想像をおこさせる「牧場」、「泉」、「落葉」、「水が澄む」等の言葉、そして「すぐ帰ってくるんだから―君も来たまえ」という、一節ごとのくり返し。

この詩を読んでから七、八年後、私はこの詩に、大学の図書館でもう一度巡り会うことになります。米詩の詩歌集（アンソロジー）の中にでもあったのでしょうか。この度は原語の英語によるものでした。この詩を、どこかで読んだことがある、と思った時、二つの節の最終行のくり返しが、記憶の中の日本語の詩と、ぴったりと重なったのです。「すぐ帰ってくるんだから―君も来たまえ。」この時初めて名前を知ったバーモントの詩人が、頁の中から呼びかけてきているようでした。

英語で読むと、更に掃除（クリーン）、落葉（リーヴス）、澄む（クリアー）、なめる（リック）、小牛（リトルカーフ）等、Ｌ音の重なりが快く思われました。しかし、こうしたことはともかくとして、この原文を読んで私が心から

感服したのは、私がかつて読んだ阿部知二[39]の日本語訳の見事さ、美しさでした。

この世界名作選を編集する時、作品を選ぶ苦心と共に、日本語の訳の苦心があった、と山本有三はその序文に記しています。既刊の翻訳に全て目を通し、カルル・ブッセの「山のあなた」の詩をのぞく、全ての作品は、悉く新たな訳者に依頼して新訳を得、又、同じ訳者の場合にも、更に良い訳を得るために加筆を求めたといいます。

私がこの本を読んだ頃、日本は既に英語を敵国語とし、その教育を禁止していました[40]。戦場におもむく学徒の携帯する本にも、さまざまな制約があったと後に聞きました。フロストやブレイクの詩も、もしこうした国の詩人の詩だと意識していたら、何らかの偏見を持って読んでいたかも知れません。

世界情勢の不安定であった一九三〇年代、四〇年代に、子供達のために、広く世界の文学を読ませたいと願った編集者があったことは、当時これらの本を手にすることの出来た日本の子供達にとり、幸いなことでした。この本を作った人々は、子供達が、まず美しいものにふれ、又、人間の悲しみ喜びに深く触れつつ、さまざまに物を思っ

20

て過ごしてほしいと願ってくれたのでしょう。因みにこの名作選の最初の数頁には、日本や世界の絵画、彫刻の写真が、黒白ではありますが載っていました。

当時私はまだ幼く、こうした編集者の願いを、どれだけ十分に受けとめていたかは分かりません。しかし、少なくとも、国が戦っていたあの暗い日々のさ中に、これらの本は国境による区別なく、人々の生きる姿そのものを私にかいま見させ、自分とは異なる環境下にある人々に対する想像を引き起こしてくれました。数冊の本と、本を私に手渡してくれた父の愛情のおかげで、私も又、世界の屋根の上にぷっかりと浮き、楽しく本を読むあのIBBYのポスターの少年の分身でいられたのです。

戦争は一九四五年の八月に終わりました。私達家族は、その後しばらく田舎にとどまり、戦災をまぬがれた東京の家にもどりました。もう小学校の最終学年になっていました。

この辺で、これまでここでとり上げてきた本の殆どが、疎開生活という、やや特殊な環境下で、私の読んだ本であったということにつき、少しふれたいと思います。

この時期、私は本当に僅かしか本を持ちませんでした。それは、数少ない本——それも、大人の手を通って来た、ある意味ではかなり教育的な本——を、普段よりもずっと集中して読んでいた、一つの特殊な期間でした。

疎開生活に入る以前、私の生活に読書がもった比重は、それ程大きなものではありません。自分の本はあまり持たず、三つ年上の兄のかなり充実した本棚に行っては、気楽で面白そうな本を選び出してきて読んでいました。私の読書力は、主に少年むきに書かれた剣豪ものや探偵小説、日本で当時ユーモア小説といわれていた、実に楽しく愉快な本の読書により得られたものです。漫画は今と違い、種類が少なかったのですが、新しいものが出ると、待ちかねて読みました。今回とり上げた「少国民文庫」にも、武井武雄[41]という人の描いた、赤ノッポ青ノッポという、二匹の鬼を主人公とする漫画がどの巻にも入っており、私はくり返しくり返しこれらを楽しみ、かなり乱暴な「鬼語」に熟達しました。

子供はまず、「読みたい」という気持から読書を始めます。ロッテンマイアーさんの指導下で少しも字を覚えなかったハイジが、クララのおばあ様から頂いた一冊の本

を読みたさに、そしてそこに、ペーターの盲目のおばあ様のために本を読んであげたい、というもう一つの動機が加わって、どんどん本が読めるようになったように。幼少時に活字に親しむことが、何より大切だと思います。ある程度の読書量に耐える力がついていなかったら、そして、急に身のまわりから消えてしまった本や活字への郷愁がなかったら、私は父が持って来てくれた数冊の本を、あれ程熱心に読むことはなかったし、一年半余におよぶ私の疎開生活に、読書の思い出をつけ加えることは出来ませんでした。

今振り返って、私にとり、子供時代の読書とは何だったのでしょう。

何よりも、それは私に楽しみを与えてくれました。そして、その後に来る、青年期の読書のための基礎を作ってくれました。

それはある時には私に根っこを与え、ある時には翼をくれました。この根っこと翼は、私が外に、内に、橋をかけ、自分の世界を少しずつ広げて育っていくときに、大きな助けとなってくれました。

読書は私に、悲しみや喜びにつき、思い巡らす機会を与えてくれました。本の中には、さまざまな悲しみが描かれており、私が、自分以外の人がどれほどに深くものを感じ、どれだけ多く傷ついているかを気づかされたのは、本を読むことによってでした。

自分とは比較にならぬ多くの苦しみ、悲しみを経ている子供達の存在を思いますと、私は、自分の恵まれ、保護されていた子供時代に、なお悲しみはあったと言うことを控えるべきかもしれません。しかしどのような生にも悲しみはあり、一人一人の子供の涙には、それなりの重さがあります。私が、自分の小さな悲しみの中で、本の中に喜びを見出せたことは恩恵でした。本の中で人生の悲しみを知ることは、自分の人生に幾ばくかの厚みを加え、他者への思いを深めますが、過去現在の作家の創作の源となった喜びに触れることは、読む者に生きる喜びを与え、失意の時に生きようとする希望を取り戻させ、再び飛翔する翼をととのえさせます。悲しみの多いこの世を子供が生き続けるためには、悲しみに耐える心が養われると共に、喜びを敏感に感じとる心、又、喜びに向かって伸びようとする心が養われることが大切だと思い

そして最後にもう一つ、本への感謝をこめてつけ加えます。読書は、人生の全てが、決して単純でないことを教えてくれました。私たちは、複雑さに耐えて生きていかなければならないということ。人と人との関係においても。国と国との関係においても。

今回お招きを頂きながら、ニューデリー会議に直接参加出来なかったことは、本当に残念なことでした。この大会を組織なさったジャファ夫人始めAWIC（Association of Writers and Illustrators for Children）の方達、IBBY会長のカルメン・デアルデン夫人、事務総長のリーナ・マイセン夫人、そして、その方達を支えたIBBYの各支部の方達にとり、この大会の開催までの道は、決してなだらかなものではなかったでしょう。皆様方は、さまざまな複雑な問題のある中で、沈着に、忍耐強く、この日を準備してこられました。その国が例えどのような政治状態にあろうとも、そこに子供達がいる限り、IBBYには果たすべき役割のあることを思い、このような形になりましたが、私はこのニューデリー大会一九九八年に参加いたしました。

どうかこれからも、これまでと同じく、本が子供の大切な友となり、助けとなることを信じ、子供達と本とを結ぶIBBYの大切な仕事をお続け下さい。

子供達が、自分の中に、しっかりとした根を持つために
子供達が、喜びと想像の強い翼を持つために
子供達が、痛みを伴う愛を知るために
そして、子供達が人生の複雑さに耐え、それぞれに与えられた人生を受け入れて生き、やがて一人一人、私共全てのふるさとであるこの地球で、平和の道具となっていくために。

《了》

皇后様とIBBYの人たち

IBB Y（国際児童図書評議会）会長　島　多代

IBBY創立者イェラ・レップマンは、第二次世界大戦中ユダヤ系であったために英国へ亡命していましたが、戦後、廃墟と化したドイツへ戻り、裸足で飢餓にむしばまれる子どもたちの精神の支えでした。「子どもたちのために、本を下さい！」と全世界に呼びかけドイツ全土で書籍展を開催し、本の必要を訴えました。人生の中で本が伝える精神の糧を知る人々が、この呼びかけに真剣に応え、一九四八年、世界中から集まった本を収録してミュンヘンに国際青少年図書館が開かれました。そして、その四年後の一九五三年、レップマンの「子どもの本を通じての国際理解」という理想の結実、「IBBY」がスイスのチューリッヒで誕生したのです。

皇后様が基調講演をなさったインド大会は、IBBY会員のための総会を含めた隔年行事のひとつでした。子どもの本について多角的観点からの講演、ストーリーテリングや人形劇公演、様々な情報交換、たとえば各地の公私図書館からの問題提起、物語、英雄伝、絵本、表現、翻訳、編集、出版、国際出版などについての討議が、充実した四日間のスケジュールにぎっしり組まれていました。皇后様の講演はプログラム第一日目の午前八時半から約一時間かけて上映されました。会場は言語も宗教も習慣も違う各国からの参加者が、ほとんど皇后様の静謐な語りに圧倒されていました。

ど全身で皇后様の言葉を受けとめていました。すべての人びとに共通な子ども時代の読書の思い出、そして今ある自分たちへの遠い日本からのこのメッセージに、深く心を揺り動かされていたようでした。

皇后様がIBBYの仕事に特に目を留められたのは、一九九〇年、世界情勢が激動し始めた頃でした。子どもたちの精神の拠り所として、本の世界を結ぶIBBYのネットワークが壊れるのを危惧されたのです。こうして当時、出版されたご著書の絵本「はじめてのやまのぼり」の印税の一部がIBBYに寄付され、大きく組み替えられていく社会変化の中で翻弄されていたIBBYに大きな希望を与えられたのです。以来、皇后様は海外への公式訪問の折、図書館、特に児童サービスの実施をしている機関を訪問される機会をもたれてきました。世界中の子どもの本の公私機関には必ずIBBYの人々が働いています。各地で皇后様をお迎えする機会を持った会員たちは皆、皇后様と不思議な絆で結ばれたと感じているようです。それは、本を手渡すことによって子どもたちに奉仕している者を励まそうとされる、そのお気持ちが伝わるからに違いありません。IBBYの人々は皇后様との一期一会を、日常の厳しい仕事の中での、貴重な励ましとして大切にしているのです。

皇后様とIBBYの人々との、いくつかの特記すべき関わりをあげてみたいと思います。一九九三年九月、詩集「どうぶつたち」(一九九二) とまど・みちお氏の新たな六十篇の翻訳が国際アンデルセン賞の国際審査員に送られ、審査が始まりました。「どうぶつたち」に含まれた二十篇に加えて全八十篇の詩の選択と翻訳は全て皇后様にお願いしました。一九九四年三月コペンハーゲンで

30

行われた審査委員会には日本の松岡享子委員をふくむ八ケ国からの児童文学者が一堂に会して厳正な審査を行い、まどさんの受賞が決まったのです。初めて詩という表現による子どもの文学が最大の評価を受けたことは世界にとっても日本にとっても意義深いことでした。世界の子どもたちに、まどさんの詩を詩と翻訳という二重の文学の枠を越えて届けることが出来ることになったからです。子どもの本の普遍的なあり方を求めてきたIBBYの人々の期待に、これほど応えた出来事は稀有なことでした。IBBYは作家、画家と共に翻訳者を宝としています。以来、皇后様はその翻訳のお仕事を通してIBBYが世界の子どもたちのために、もっとも誇り得る且つ期待を寄せる方となられたのです。

ミュンヘンの国際青少年図書館を訪ねられたのは、一九九三年の秋、当地では「日本絵本歴史展」が開催されていました。現在の絵本を中心に絵巻から始まる日本の絵本の歴史を紹介したIBBY日本支部（JBBY）のこの企画展は、チューリッヒで開幕し、ドイツを経て、パリの国立図書館で幕を閉じることになっていました。質素な中世の古城跡を利用して建てられた国際青少年図書館は、IBBY創立の先駆けとなった子どもの本研究の中心です。ここで皇后様をお迎えしたシャリオット館長は一九八六年から理事としてIBBYに深く関わっています。また、同席したドイツのアンデルセン賞候補画家ビネッテ・シュレーダーは、何年を経ても皇后様との出会いが忘れられないと語ります。そして、自分のあの時の感動を筆に託して必ず表現するのだ、と。

パリ郊外のクラマール児童図書館を訪れられたのは一九九四年でした。低所得者階層の住居の集

まるこの地域での児童図書サービスをじかにご覧になる機会となりました。ここで皇后様をお迎えしたのは、市立児童書資料館「本の喜び」を主宰するパット館長と、バーゼルから駆けつけたIBBYのリーナ事務局長でした。二人とも子どもの本の国際ネットワークのために優に二五年の年月を捧げてきた人達です。

米国議会図書館の児童書センターも皇后様をお迎え出来た喜びを忘れえないでいます。ここでは一九八七年に所蔵している日本の児童図書から三〇〇冊を選び、その歴史と概要を目録として出版し、シンポジウム「日本の窓」を開催しました。以来皇后様にはセンターの案内状をお送りし続けてきました。一九九四年、ワシントンご訪問の際、児童書センターで、ヤグッシュ博士とコーラン女史の説明で聞かれたアメリカ児童文学史のあらすじは、皇后様の米国理解に何らかのお役にたったものと思われます。戦後石井桃子さんが渡米されて、「ポストの数ほどの」と表現された米国の公立図書館を束ねるこの小さなセンターを皇后様は丁寧に見て下さった、と喜びの報告を聞きました。ご著書「ANIMALS」の出版元マッケルダリー・ブックスのマッケルダリー女史も重要な著者の御来訪に高齢をおしてニューヨークから大使館のレセプションに出席しました。たった三〇秒の、しかし忘れがたい印象を刻まれ、マーガレット女史は翌春に日本来訪をはたしました。これらの人々は、言うまでもなく米国IBBYの大切な担い手たちなのです。

今年六月、IBBY朝日児童図書普及賞を記念するシンポジウム「本を下さい！翼を下さい！」が開かれました。シンポジウムに参加したヴェネズエラ「本の銀行」のデアルデン女史はI

BBY前会長、インド「AWIC」のジャファ夫人は第二六回IBBYインド大会実行委員長、タイ「移動図書館」のシンカマナン夫人はタイIBBY支部長です。日本の「ふれあい文庫」(点字絵本)の岩田美津子さんを含めて参加者は全員、IBBY朝日賞の受賞者でした。ご来場くださった皇后様は、ロバやラクダの背に積んで僻地の子どもたちのもとに本を運んでいる人達、一五〇〇もの言語を持つインドの識字問題などの活動に携わる人々など、IBBYとの新たな出会いの時を持たれました。

いつも、いかに子どもたちに本を手渡すかを考え、お母さんや先生たち子どもたちに奉仕する人達を支えるIBBYの仕事は厳しく地味です。しかし、その仕事の重要性は社会の未来に関わることなので、一度始めたら止めるわけにはいきません。そのような人びとが世界中で黙々と仕事をし続けていることを、知っていて下さる皇后様の存在が、如何に大きく貴重か、言葉で言い表わすことはとても出来ません。

第二六回IBBYインド大会に於ける皇后様のご講演に対し、IBBY会員を代表してここに深く、感謝いたします。

注

1 アルプスのハイジ
スイスのヨハンナ・シュピーリ (Johanna Spyri, 1829–1901) 作 *Heidi* (1881) の主人公。邦訳に『ハイジ』矢川澄子訳 福音館書店、『ハイジ上・下』竹山道雄訳 岩波書店などがある。

2 モーグリ少年
英国のラディヤード・キプリング (Rudyard Kipling, 1865–1936) 作 *The Jungle Book* (1894) の主人公。邦訳に『ジャングル・ブック』木島始訳 福音館書店など。

3 エッツの男の子
アメリカの絵本作家マリー・ホール・エッツ (Marie Hall Ets, 1893–1984) の代表作 *In the Forest* (1944) の主人公。邦訳は『もりのなか』まさきるりこ訳 福音館書店。

4 レオ・レオーニの「あおくん」や「きいろちゃん」
オランダ出身の絵本作家レオ・レオーニ (Leo Lionni, 1910–) 作 *Little Blue and Little Yellow* (1959) の主人公。邦訳は『あおくんときいろちゃん』藤田圭雄訳 至光社。

5 バートンの『ちいさいおうち』
アメリカの絵本作家バージニア・リー・バートン (Virginia Lee Burton, 1909–1968) 作 *The Little House* (1942) の主人公。邦訳はいしいももこ訳 岩波書店。

6 トールキン John Ronald Reuel Tolkien, 1892–1973
英国の作家。オックスフォード大学で英語英文学教授として教鞭をとるかたわら、著作活動に

入る。代表作に *The Hobbit ; or, There and Back Again*, 1937『ホビットの冒険』瀬田貞二訳 岩波書店、*The Lord of the Rings*, 1954〜55『指輪物語』全6巻 瀬田貞二・田中明子訳 評論社がある。

7 C・S・ルイス Clive Staples Lewis, 1898-1963
英国の学者、批評家、小説家。子ども向けの代表作に *The Chronicles of Narnia*, 1950-1956『ナルニア国ものがたり』全7巻 瀬田貞二訳 岩波書店がある。

8 ローズマリー・サトクリフ Rosemary Sutcliff, 1920-1992
英国の児童文学作家、小説家。代表作に *Warrior Scarlet*, 1958『太陽の戦士』猪熊葉子訳 岩波書店、*The Lantern Bearers*, 1959『ともしびをかかげて』猪熊葉子訳 岩波書店などの歴史物語がある。

9 フィリッパ・ピアス Ann Philippa Pearce, 1920-
英国の児童文学作家。代表作に *Tom's Midnight Garden*, 1958『トムは真夜中の庭で』高杉一郎訳 岩波書店がある。

10 新美南吉（1913-1943）
自筆原稿「デンデンムシノカナシミ」は一九三五年（昭和十年）作。友人巽聖歌によって、南吉の死後一九五〇年（昭和二十五年）に初めて単行本とされ、一九八〇年（昭和五十五年）発行の『校定・新美南吉全集』（大日本図書）にも収録されているが、それ以前の発表ルートについては現在のところ確認されていない。なお『あかいろうそく』（一九七三年 大日本図書）にも収録されている。

11 カレワラ Kalevala

12 オシーン Oisin (Ossian)
フィンランドの民族叙事詩。一八三五年にエリアス・レンロートがはじめて本の形で出版、一九六六年にマルッティ・ハーヴィオが散文形式の「カレワラ物語」を出版した。後者を底本とした邦訳に『カレワラタリナ』坂井玲子訳 第三文明社がある。

13 リヤ Ler (Lir)
アイルランドの伝説の海の神。その子どもたちをめぐる物語は「リアの子供たち」として『アイルランドの神話伝説Ⅰ』（八住利雄編 名著普及会）に「アイルランドの神話伝説Ⅱ』（八住利雄編 名著普及会）に「アイルランドの民話と伝説』（三宅忠明著 大修館書店）に収録されている。ゲール語での発音は「リル」に近く、英語では「リア」「リヤ」のように発音されている。

14 ラマヤナ Ramayana
古代インドの大叙事詩「ラーマ王行伝」の意。伝本は四種あるが、最も古いといわれる「ボンベイ本」を底本とした邦訳に『ラーマーヤナ1、2』ヴァールミーキ著 岩本裕訳 平凡社、他に物語風の抄訳『ラーマーヤナ上・下』河田清史著 第三文明社などがある。

15 ジャータカ Jataka
古代インドの仏教説話集。ブッダがこの世に生まれてくる以前の功徳を語る前世物語。邦訳に『ジャータカ物語1〜5』中村元・増谷文雄監修 鈴木出版、子ども向けには『ジャータカ物語』辻直四郎・渡辺照宏共訳 岩波書店がある。

16　ポポル・ブフ　Popul Vuh

メキシコのマヤ文化の聖典。邦訳に『ポポル・ヴフ』A・レシーノス原訳・校注　林屋永吉訳　中央公論社がある。

17　「子供の本の日」

アンデルセンの誕生日である四月二日を「子供の本の日」と定め、IBBYに加盟している各国で一九六七年以来行事を行い、各国が持ちまわりでポスターとメッセージを発表している。

18　倭建御子

19　「古事記」「日本書紀」「風土記」などに伝えられる英雄伝説の主人公。

日本少国民文庫

一九三五年（昭和10年）に新潮社より刊行された叢書全16巻。内容は科学・文芸・歴史などにわたる。

皇后様は、この全集をこの時以降中学時代全般にわたり愛読され、平成六年、フランス御訪問に先立つ記者会見の中では、この全集につき、次のようにお触れになっている。

「フランスに対して持つ興味の元をたどってまいりますと、中学生の頃に読んだ小国民文庫の数冊が思い出されます。ジャン・クリストフの中の一章、シャルル・フィリップの母への手紙、フランシス・ジャムの短い詩などが載せられていました。また、黒白の印刷ではありましたが、フランスの絵画が紹介されており、こうした絵をずっと後に色ずりの画集の中で見た時の喜びは、大きなものでした。私のフランスへの興味は、少女時代に得たこの小さな土台の上に、少しずつ育っていったものではないかと考えています。」

20　「リッキ・ティキ・タヴィー物語」Rikki-Tikki-Tavi

21 キブリングの「ジャングル・ブック」(訳注②参照) 中の一話。邦訳『ジャングル・ブック』西村孝次訳 学習研究社に収録されている。

22 英国の作家 Oscar Wilde (1854-1900) の作品。原題 *The Happy Prince*, 1888。邦訳『幸福な王子』西村孝次訳 新潮文庫などがある。ワイルドの「幸福の王子」西村孝次訳 新潮文庫に収録されている。

23 チェコの劇作家、小説家、ジャーナリスト Karel Čapek (1890-1938) の作品。原題 *Devatero Pohadeck Karla Capka*『長い長いお医者さんの話』中野好夫訳 岩波書店にも「郵便屋さんの話」として収録されている。カレル・チャペックの「郵便配達の話」

24 トルストイ (レフ・H・Ники olievicz・トルストイ лев H. Толстой, 1828-1910) ロシアの作家。代表作に『アンナ・カレーニナ』(1875-78)。「人は何によって生きるか」は、子ども向けの邦訳『イワンのばか』金子幸彦訳 岩波書店、『トルストイの民話』藤沼貴訳 福音館書店にも収録されている。

25 チェーホフ (アントン・パヴロヴィチ Антон П. Чехов 1860-1904) ロシアの作家。代表作に『かもめ』(1896)、『ワーニャ伯父さん』(1897) などがある。

26 シャルル・ルイ・フィリップ Charles-Louis Philippe, 1874-1909 フランスの作家。代表作に『母と子』(1900) がある。

アメリカの詩人、エッセイスト。代表作に *The Gift from the Sea*, 1955 邦訳『海からの贈物』吉田健一訳 新潮社また落合恵子訳 立風書房がある。アン・モロー・リンドバーグ Anne Morrow Lindbergh, 1906–

27 ケストナー（エーリヒ） Erich Kästner, 1899–1974
ドイツの詩人、小説家。子ども向きの作品には *Emil und die Detektive*, 1929 邦訳『エーミールと探偵たち』高橋健二訳 岩波書店などがある。

28 マーク・トウェイン Mark Twain, 1835–1910
アメリカの作家。子ども向きの作品では、*The Adventures of Tom Sawyer* 1876 邦訳『トム・ソーヤの冒険』、*The Adventures of Huckleberry Finn* 1884 邦訳『ハックルベリー・フィンの冒険上・下』石井桃子訳 岩波書店、大塚勇三訳 福音館書店がある。

29 ロマン・ロラン Romain Rolland, 1866–1944
フランスの作家。代表作に『ジャン・クリストフ』(1904–12) などがある。

30 ヘンリー・ヴァンダイク Henry Van Dyke, 1852–1933
アメリカの宗教家。子ども向きの物語に *The Story of the Other Wise Man* (1896) がある。

31 ラスキン（ジョン） John Ruskin, 1819–1900
英国の美術評論家、社会思想家。唯一の児童文学作品に *The King of the Golden River* (1851) 邦訳『黄金の川の王さま』小野章訳 講談社がある。

32 カルル・ブッセ Karl Busse, 1872–1917
ドイツの詩人、小説家。代表作「青春の嵐」(1896) がある。

33 フランシス・ジャム Francis Jammes, 1868–1938
フランスの詩人。代表作に「明けの鐘から夕べの鐘まで」(1898) がある。

34 ウィリアム・ブレイク William Blake, 1757–1827
イギリスロマン派の先駆的な詩人。画家、彫刻家でもある。詩集に『無垢の歌』(1789) ほか

がある。

35 ロバート・フロスト Robert Lee Frost, 1874-1963 アメリカの詩人。代表作に「草刈り」(1914)がある。ピューリッツァー賞を4回受賞。

36 タゴール（ラビンドラナート）Rabindranāth Tagore, 1861-1941 インドのベンガル語詩人、小説家、教育者。一九一三年東洋人として初めてノーベル賞受賞、作品の邦訳に『タゴール著作集』全12巻第三文明社がある。

37 ソログーブ（フョードル）Фёдор Сологуб 1863-1927 ロシアの作家。ロシア象徴派の代表。児童文学作品として『金色の柱』『影絵』などがある。
（＊ソログープという表記が一般的）

38 山本有三 (1887-1974) 小説家、劇作家。栃木県生れ。小説『波』『真実一路』『路傍の石』などがある。

39 阿部知二 (1903-1973) 小説家。岡山県生れ。『冬の宿』『風雪』などがある。

40 戦争中の英語教育については様々な実態があったようであるが、平凡社世界大百科事典（初版）の「英語」の項中「日本における英語教育」には、太平洋戦争突入以後の英語教育につき、「…あるいはその授業時間をへらされ、あるいは全廃されて敗戦の日にいたった」と記されている。

今回本書を作成するにあたり、皇后さまは、本文のこの箇所に注釈を付し、戦時下の文部省通達は、英語教育の「禁止」ではなく、授業時数などの「規制」であった旨を明記するよう御依頼になった。

41 武井武雄（1894-1983）
童画家、版画家。童話に「ラムラム王」(1926)、長編漫画に「赤ノッポ青ノッポ」(1934)などがある。

42 平和の道具
アッシジのフランシスコ作といわれ、世界的に知られた『平和のための祈り』の冒頭の一節、「我をして御身の平和の道具とならしめ給え」を指す。

＊ ビデオ講演では「二十五歳」となっているが、皇后さまは収録後にこの部分の間違いに気付かれ、原稿を「二十六歳」と訂正された。この一九六〇年に、皇后さまは皇太子妃として米国及びインドを含む中近東、アジア、アフリカと、二度にわたる外国公式訪問をしておられ、この二つのご旅行の短い合間に二十六歳のお誕生日を迎えられている。

注の作成については「財団法人東京子ども図書館」の協力をいただきました。

IBBYニューデリー大会の皇后様による基調講演は、収録にあたりこれを英語でとるか、日本語でとり英語の字幕を付すかは編集段階まで決定しませんでした。最終的にはインドでは英語版を使うこととなりましたが、収録にあたってきたNHKはこの段階でご講演の内容を惜しみ、国内でもこれを放送できないものかと宮内庁に許可を求め、ビデオは日本語版、英語版共に宮内庁を通じ、全テレビ局に渡されることになりました。放映は大きな反響を呼び、是非書物で読みたいとの要望も多く、ここにそのご講演を出版いたします。

India where hundreds of languages and dialects are spoken.

Devoted to finding ways to put books in the hands of children and to support the efforts of people serving children, their parents and teachers, the work of IBBY is perennially difficult and not particularly well-known. It is work, nonetheless, that will make a difference in the future, and having committed ourselves to it, we cannot abandon our mission. It is difficult to express in words how great and precious is the presence of Empress Michiko, who knows and supports the often unrecognized endeavours of people like these all over the world.

On behalf of the membership of IBBY, I would like to express our profound gratitutde to the Empress for her inspiring speech for the 26 th IBBY Congress in New Delhi. (translated by Lynne Riggs)

March 1999

Eager to welcome an honoured translator to the United States, Margaret McElderry, whose publishing house brought out *The Animals*, travelled to Washington from New York to attend the reception for the Emperor and Empress held at the Embassy of Japan. The barely thirty-second meeting with the Empress left an indelible impression on McElderry, inspiring her to visit Japan the following spring.

In June 1998, a symposium commemorating the twelfth year of the IBBY-Asahi Reading Promotion Award, "Give Us Books, Give Us Wings", was held in Tokyo. Panelists included four previous award winners : Carmen Diana Dearden, then President of IBBY and representative of the Banco del Libro of Venezuela, ; Manorama Jafa. Secretary General of the Association of Writers and Illustrators for Children of India and chairperson of the 26th IBBY Congress in New Delhi ; Somboon Singkamanan, founder of the Portable Library Project of Thailand and also head of the Thai Section of IBBY, as well as Mitsuko Iwata, founder-director of the Fureai Bunko Braille Picture Book Library.

The Empress attended the Symposium, hearing the participants' accounts, such as of how books are carried by donkey or camel over perilous terrain to children in remote areas, and of the problems of people working with literacy and other programmes in a country like library and the well-known children's book institution La Joie par les Livres, and IBBY's Executive Director Leena Maissen, who had come from Basel. Both are people who have devoted themselves to building the children's book network for more than a quarter of a century.

The opportunity to welcome the Empress at the time of her visit to the Children's Literature Center at the Library of Congress in Washington was also unforgettable. Several years earlier, in 1987, the Center had chosen 300 titles from its collection of Japanese children's books, published a list outlining their history, and held a symposium entitled "Windows on Japan". From that time they had regularly sent the Empress information about the activities of the Center, and during an official visit to Washington in 1994, she was able to visit the Center, where Dr. Sybille Jagusch and Ms. Margaret N. Coughlan presented an outline of the history of American children's literature, which must have helped the Empress understand the situation in the United States better. The Center serves the vast network of public libraries throughout the United States, which Momoko Ishii, who travelled to the United States shortly after World War II, was amazed to find are "as numerous as post boxes". The staff reported to me how delighted they were about the attention given by the Empress to their small Center.

since that time, Empress Michiko has become for IBBY a highly esteemed associate.

The Empress visited the International Youth Library in Munich for the first time in the fall of 1993, when an exhibition on the history of Japanese picture books, sponsored by the Japanese Board on Books for Young People, was being held. This exhibition, introducing the history of the picture book in Japan from the picture scrolls of ancient times to the present, opened in Zurich and toured Germany, closing after a show at the Bibliothèque Nationale, Paris. The International Youth Library, housed in a renovated mediaeval castle, is the centre of children's books that led to the founding of IBBY. The Empress was met on her visit to the Library by its director, Dr. Barbara Scharioth, who has long been deeply involved with IBBY. German illustrator and Andersen Award nominee Binette Schroeder, who was also present on that occasion, recalls that she will never forget her encounter with the Empress. She says that some day she will certainly write and draw about her memorable impressions of that experience.

In 1994. the Empress visited the Bibliothèque des Enfants et Jeunes in the suburb of Clamart outside Paris, giving her an opportunity to observe children's library services in a low-income residential community. There she was met by Geneviève Patte, head of the books in the hands of children. I believe that many people of IBBY who have met the Empress deeply treasure the sincere encouragement she extends to them in their daily work.

Let me introduce here some of the particularly memorable occasions that illustrate the close relationship between IBBY and Empress Michiko. In 1993, Japanese poet Michio Mado was nominated as a candidate for the Hans Christian Andersen Writer's Award. Materials including a volume of Mado's poems, translated by the Empress, and published in 1992 as *The Animals*, as well as 60 newly translated poems were forwarded to the international jury. The Jury met in Copenhagen in March 1994: specialists in children's literature from ten countries, including Kyoko Matsuoka from Japan. They chose Michio Mado as the winner.

This highest recognition, the first for work in the genre of poetry for children, was significant both for the world and for Japan. It meant that the magic of Mado's poetry had been successfully brought to the children of the world, transcending the boundaries of both poetry and translation. In the search for what is universal in books for children, few events have so well fulfilled the expectations of IBBY members. For IBBY, writers, illustrators, and translators are precious treasures, and evoked so many memories that those present shared, and by the eloquence of her message spoken from Japan, far away from where they were assembled.

Empress Michiko first became interested in the work of IBBY in 1990. At a time when the world was in the throes of tumultuous changes in the wake of the end of the Cold War, she became concerned that difficulties with funding might cause the collapse of the global network that IBBY had created to give children a spiritual refuge through books. She donated to IBBY part of the royalties from her picture book entitled *Hajimete no yamanobori* (My first mountain climbing), Shikosa 1991. This support provided great hope to IBBY at a time of social upheaval and change.

From that time onward, each time that the Empress travelled abroad on official business, she began to enjoy opportunities to visit libraries, especially those offering services in children's books. Many of the people who make up IBBY work in both public and private children's libraries throughout the world, and those who have had occasion to meet the Empress on one of these visits invariably remark about the special bond that they feel links them with the Empress, who shares with them a deep devotion to books and children. Certainly that bond is established by the strength of her desire to encourage them in their work of putting

In 1948, the International Youth Library was opened in Munich, housing the books that had been collected from all over the world in response to Lepman's call. Five years later, in 1953, the International Board on Books for Young People (IBBY) was founded in Zurich to pursue her ideal of "Seeking international understanding through books for children".

The biennial Congress and General Assembly held in New Delhi in September 1998 was a major event for IBBY. The four days of the Congress were scheduled with a dense and rich succession of lectures and meetings, storytelling sessions, puppet play performances, and a variety of information exchange events. There were symposia and workshops on problems shared by public and private libraries in various parts of the world, as well as sessions on classics of world literature, picture books, different forms of expression, translation, editing, publishing, international co-production, and many other topics.

The Congress opened with the keynote speech given by Empress Michiko of Japan, shown by video on a large screen. One could see that everyone in the hall was listening intently to the Empress's quietly spoken words. Though the participants came from diverse linguistic, religious, and cultural backgrounds, all were deeply moved by her reminiscencies of reading as a child that

The Empress Michiko of Japan and the Members of IBBY

Tayo Shima
President
International Board on Books for Young People

IBBY's founder Jella Lepman, being of Jewish origin, sought refuge in England during World War II. When it was over, she returned to Germany, and there saw firsthand the misery of children left barefoot and hungry in the wake of war. They lacked food and shelter, she observed, but the children of war also needed sustenance that would nurture their minds and spirits. And with this in mind, she launched her movement, appealing to the world to "Give Us Books", holding book displays throughout Germany, and urging people to see the need for books for children. Many people cognizant of the spiritual nourishment that books give to people's lives contributed to and committed themselves to this appeal.

in a country, as long as there are children, IBBY has a role to carry out, I have participated, although in this manner, in this New Delhi Congress '98. Please continue, as you have done up to now, IBBY's important work of linking books and children, in the belief that books are children's valuable friends and are a help to them:

So that children have firm roots within themselves;

So that children have strong wings of joy and of imagination;

So that children know love, accepting that at times love calls for pain;

So that children see and face the challenge of life's complexities, fully taking on the life given to each, and finally, upon this earth which is our common home, become, one day, true instruments of peace.

own life and deepens one's thought for others. Similarly, coming in touch with joy in books—the joy that was the wellspring of creative works by writers past and present—imparts the joy of living to the reader, and when at times he is overcome by helplessness, may help restore his hope in life, providing wings for him to take flight once again. In order that children may cope with life in this world of sorrows, as well as preparing them to endure sorrows, I think it is so important to foster in them hearts susceptible to joy, hearts sensitively turned to joy.

I would like to add one more thing, including my gratitude to books. Reading taught me that life is surely not a simple thing. We must recognize and face life's complexity. In person to person relations. In country to country relations, too.

It is truly regrettable that, having received your kind invitation, I cannot attend this New Delhi Congress in person. For you, the organizers of the Congress—Chairperson Mrs. Manorama Jafa and the members of AWIC, IBBY President Mrs. Carmen Dearden, General Secretary Mrs. Leena Maissen, and your supporters, the members of the various IBBY branches—the way to this 26th Congress was surely not a smooth and easy road. Yet, beset by many complicated problems, with composure and unflagging perseverance you continued preparations for this day. Believing that whatever be the political situation and if I did not feel nostalgic for the books and printed word that suddenly were gone from round me, I would not have been able to add reading to my memories of my evacuation life of more than one year and a half.

Looking back on it now, what did my childhood reading do for me?

Above all, it gave me pleasure and then laid the foundation for my later reading during adolescence.

At times it gave me roots; at times it gave me wings. These roots and wings were a great help to me as I threw bridges out and in, expanding bit by bit and nurturing my own personal world.

Reading gave me opportunities to ponder over joy and sorrow. It was through reading books, with the many kinds of grief delineated in them, that I could come to know how deeply people other than myself can feel, or that I could perceive the many hurts they bear.

When I think that there are children who go through so many griefs and pains beyond comparison with mine, maybe I should refrain from saying that in my own sheltered childhood, too, there were such things as sorrows. But, in any life whatever, there is pain and sorrow. The tears of every single child have their specific weight. For me, when I was caught up in my own small sorrows, it was a blessing to be able to find joy in books. Learning of life's sorrows adds to some extent more depth to one's have many books of my own. I used to freely go to the fairly well-stocked bookshelves of my brother, three years older than myself, and pick out whatever book looked interesting. My reading ability was acquired thus, mostly through books written with young boys in mind: stories of master-swordsmen, detective stories, and what were called in the Japan of those days humour novels, which were both amusing and delightful. Unlike the present time, there was no great variety of comics then, so when a new one would come out, I could hardly wait to read it. Even in the 'Library of Books for the Younger Generation' that I have cited, every volume came with a comic supplement, the cartoons drawn by an artist with the name of Takei Takeo. The heroes were two thunder-devils, Red the Tall and Green the Tall. I read those comics over and over again with the greatest pleasure, and soon became quite proficient in their rough and rude vocabulary of devil-speak.

A child starts reading, first of all, when it feels 'I want to read.' Just like Heidi—who could not learn her letters at all under Fräulein Rottenmeier's guidance—through wanting so much to read the book Clara's grandmother had given her, and with the other additional motivation of wanting to read it to Peter's blind grandmother, was soon able to read any book she liked. It is so important to familiarize oneself with print at an early age. If I had not been able to stand up to a certain amount of reading, pages photographs of Japanese and world paintings and sculptures, although only in black and white.

Being a child at the time, I am not sure to what degree I was able to take in the editors' desires, but at least, right in the middle of the dark days when our country was at war, those books, without distinction of national borders, raised my imagination so that I could get a glimpse of just how other people lived in life environments different from my own. Thanks to a few books and my father's love, I was the *alter ego* of the boy in IBBY's poster, happily reading as he floated airily above the world's roofs.

The war came to an end in August 1945. Our family stayed on in the country for a little while, and then came home to our Tokyo house, which had escaped war damage. It was already my last year of elementary school.

At this point, I would like to revert to the fact that nearly all the books I have mentioned up to now were books I read in a quite unique environment, during the evacuation.

At that time, I had only a few books. Those books, few in number—which had come to me through the hands of adults and were in a sense quite educational—I read with far more than usual concentration in what was a very special period.

Before entering on my life as an evacuee, the relative importance of my reading was not so very great. I did not troubles involving the Japanese translations. He looked through all previously published versions of the pieces and, with the exception of Karl Busse's 'Far Beyond the Mountains', he requested new translators to do fresh versions of everything. Also, in certain cases where he retained the same translators, in order to obtain a still finer version, he required them to do a revision of their work.

At the time I read this poem, education in English was proscribed because it was the language of the enemy. I heard later that there were also certain restrictions on the books that could be carried by students leaving for the battlefront. I myself, child that I was, unequivocally thought of Britain and the United States as the enemy. The poetry of Frost and Blake—if I had realized that these poets belonged to those countries, perhaps I would have read them with some bias.

In the 1930s and 1940s, when the world was in such an unsettled state, it was most fortunate for the children of Japan who could get these books that there were editors who wanted them to be widely read in world literature. The people who compiled the books must have been impelled first of all by a desire to have children come in touch with beauty, and again, they must have wanted to incite children to ponder many things, as they came deeply in touch with the sorrows and the joys of human beings. Incidentally, the books had in their first

I cannot adequately explain in what consists this poem's source of joy. Of course, the poem's content imparts a pleasant feeling, but in the words here used, a number of mysteries seem to lie concealed: words that lead to delight, such as 'pasture', 'spring', 'leaves', 'water clear', and the refrain that winds up each stanza, 'I shan't be gone long. —You come too.'

Some seven or eight years after I first read this poem, I came across it again, this time in English, in the university library. Would it have been in an anthology of American poetry? Just as it occurred to me that I had read the poem before somewhere, I saw that the refrain in the last line of both stanzas fitted exactly over the same two lines in the Japanese version which now came back to me. Robert Frost, the poet of Vermont whose name I first learnt through this poem, seemed to be calling out to *me* from the page.

When I read the poem in English, I took even greater delight in the words, like the accumulation of liquid 'L' sounds in 'clean', 'leaves', 'clear', 'lick', 'little calf', and so on. Be that as it may, however, what stirred my heart with wonder and admiration, even as I read the original, were the excellence and beauty of Abe Tomoji's Japanese translation that I had read so long before.

Yamamoto Yūzō in his preface says that when editing the 'Masterpieces of World Literature', apart from difficulties in selecting suitable works, there were also over, it seemed to set my heart dancing. Within this rhythmic frame, which the Japanese have loved from ancient times, the very words seemed to glow and sparkle, luminous with felicity. This was when I glimpsed for the first time the delight and exaltation that poetry can give to people's hearts. Earlier, I spoke about the 'root' that books had given me, but the 'joy' I have here described, together with the powers of imagination I will now touch upon, are for me like mighty 'wings' that let my heart go soaring to the heights.

The editor of 'Masterpieces of World Literature', together with sad poems that made the spirit sink, did not forget to select poems that made the heart dance for joy. One of the poems which gave me that kind of joy was a translation of Robert Frost's 'The Pasture'. Since it is a short poem, I will read it.

THE PASTURE

I'm going out to clean the pasture spring;
I'll only stop to rake the leaves away
(And wait to watch the water clear, I may):
I shan't be gone long. —You come too.

I'm going out to fetch the little calf
That's standing by the mother. It's so young
It totters when she licks it with her tongue.
I shan't be gone long. —You come too.

life would last? And also, did he perhaps feel he wanted children to learn, like the little snail in the story, that everyone has his own burden of sorrows?

Apart from two or three of his novels and plays, I know little of Yamamoto Yūzō who planned the general outline for this series. However, as regards the editing of 'Masterpieces of Japanese Literature' and 'Masterpieces of World Literature', I cannot help but feel that Yūzō and his collaborators were impelled by a strong desire to have children taste both joy and sorrow to their depths.

Let me now talk rather about joy, the joy I got from books. To be sure, learning that so many kinds of grief are to be found all round us sometimes made my heart grow heavy, plunging it in gloom. But children have a strange resilience that rights their balance. Thus, at the same time that I was saddened by my vicarious experience through books of the sorrows of this life, similarly, in books I was discovering great joys that made my spirits move in a most lively way, making something like gratitude for being alive well up in me. Might I call it a sensation of delight?

The first time I got this perception was in those war days, when I came upon a tanka poem in a little book my father had in his bag. It was a lovely poem heralding the coming of Spring, composed in the conventional form of 5/7/5/7/7 syllables, and as I read it over and worry, so she goes out to look for him and finds him there. 'Wherever have you been?' she asks him, but the child just bursts out sobbing and crying. 'His suffering was greater than his mother's love:/Sunk in dejection, they both went into the house.' With these words the poem ends.

In the 'Masterpieces of World Literature' selection, apart from this 'First Despair', there was another sad story by the Russian writer Sologub called 'Body-search'. It is a story of a child from a poor home who is suspected of theft at school. He is made to undergo a thorough search of his person: his pockets, his socks, and even under his clothes. While this is going on, the stolen article turns up elsewhere, and he is cleared of suspicion. This day, when he gets home, his mother listens attentively to all he has to tell, and then makes the bleak rejoinder: 'Ah, you can't say anything. Remember, when you grow up, you'll have to face far worse than *that*. In this world anything can happen, you know!'

I remember that, during the war, in order to raise the people's spirits, stirring tales of valour were the usual fare. In such a situation, why the editor of this series chose to include pieces like 'The First Despair' and 'Body-search' is a matter of deep interest to me.

Is it that he thought it necessary, from a certain time in their lives, to prepare children to face the many inescapable griefs they would be troubled with as long as

Orient'. The names of such as Erich Kästner, Mark Twain, Romain Rolland, Henry Van Dyke and John Ruskin also appear. As proof that I had not necessarily read everything carefully, there are places where I have only a vague memory of the content.

There were also some poems of a level that children could understand.

Karl Busse, Francis Jammes, William Blake, Robert Frost . . . and also it was from the pages of this book that I first learnt the name of India's poet Rabindranath Tagore. His poem 'The Flower-School' was one of the selections. In later years, what was my joy when I rediscovered it in his collection titled 'The Crescent Moon'! There, 'The Flower-School' led me straight away to other poems of the same poet: 'Baby's Way', 'The Judge', 'The Champa Flower'.

Erich Kästner's 'The First Despair' was an excessively sad poem. A little boy, with a one-mark coin tightly clutched in his sweaty fist, goes trotting off to buy some bread and bacon. All of a sudden he notices that the money he had in his fist is gone. One after another, the show-window lights go out, and everywhere the shops are closing doors. The boy's father and mother, tired out after a long day's work, are waiting for their child's return. That child has come as far as the house, turned his face to the wall, and goes on standing there perfectly still. The mother, who does not know this, begins to them for me. All three were in a series called 'Library of Books for the Younger Generation'. This series was comprised of some fifteen or sixteen volumes, with titles such as 'What Has Man Achieved?'; 'People Devoted to Serving Human Progress'; 'Stories of Great Inventions—Scientific and Practical'; or 'Sports and Adventure Stories', systematically arranged volume by volume. The books of the series which Father brought me at that time were 'Masterpieces of Japanese Literature' in one volume, and 'Masterpieces of World Literature' in two volumes.

This series was first published in 1936, when my brother was five and I was just two. Later, during the war, a revised edition came out in 1942. Judging from my brother's age, the books, bought for him by my mother, would, I think, have been of this revised edition. The volumes I now have at hand are copies of the 1936 first edition that reached me over ten years ago. The contents in them of the 'Masterpieces' practically coincide with my memories of them, so that it may be assumed there was little or no alteration between the pre-war and wartime editions.

Of the three books, when I now open the two volumes of 'Masterpieces of World Literature', I find such selections as Kipling's 'Rikki-Tikki-Tavi' from 'The Jungle Book'; Oscar Wilde's 'The Happy Prince'; Karel Čapek's 'A Postman's Story'; Tolstoy's 'What Men Live By'; letters of Charles Philippe and of Chekhov, and the Japan travels related in Anne Morrow Lindbergh's 'North to the simply very close but rather were inseparable, two facets of one selfsame thing.

It was for me a strange experience. I continued to be drawn to this story for its beauty, but at the same time it oppressed me with a nameless sense of unease.

Now no longer ancient times, in our own day the thought that calming stormy seas could be done by calling for the sacrifice of someone's life is inconceivable. Therefore, human sacrifice is something that I had no need to fear. But I then felt there was some timeless symbolism in Oto-Tachibana's story, something that made my breathing difficult. When I think about it now, I see that it may be because the thing called love can sometimes take severe and cruel-seeming forms, and my unease may well have been my awe and fear of that indivisibility of love and sacrifice that I have described.

Because I was still just a child, I felt everything in only a vague and confused way, and this sense of choking that I could not understand ran together with the image from the story of sinking under water, and I remember being perturbed by this old tale for quite some time.

Along with the books my father had himself chosen for me in those evacuation days were three others that he brought me which still stay in my memory. These belonged to my elder brother, and I had been wanting to read them sometime, so I had asked my father to borrow

Some time before this, while Takeru and Oto-Tachibana were crossing a withered plain, their enemy devised a cruel stratagem of setting fire to the grass, leaving them engulfed in raging flames, fleeing this way and that, in peril of their lives. Oto-Tachibana's poem, meaning 'You my Lord who at that time, in the middle of the raging fires, showed such thought for *my* safety', was composed in a spirit of gratitude for the tender solicitude shown towards her by the Prince in his own hour of gravest danger.

Even before this, I already knew a few sad 'sacrifice' stories. However, the 'victim' in this story was somewhat different. Oto-Tachibana's words and actions—how can I best express this?—imply that she was fully associating herself with Takeru's mission: somewhere one senses inference of a firm, conscious will. Oto-Tachibana's poem—I cannot now rightly remember whether it was given in a modern rendering or in the original Old Japanese with explanations attached—seemed to me a thing of surpassing beauty. In this poem she made as she faced the cruel fate of sacrificial victim, taken on, moreover, by her own self, she no doubt sang the moment of her life which she remembered as overflowing with the greatest love and gratitude. Rather than a deep impression, its effect on me was a strong shock. Although I could not put it into precise words, somewhere inside me I got the perception that love and sacrifice were not

Takeru no Miko (The Prince-Brave of Yamato)—whenever he made an expedition to a remote area, by command of his father the Emperor, to put down a rebellion, having succeeded in subjugating the rebels, would make a triumphal return. But his Emperor father, as if he felt threatened by the power of his son, would then command him to go forth on yet another mission, without giving him the slightest rest or respite. His heart wrapped round with sadness, the Prince set out once more on what was to be his last campaign of putting down rebellion. On the way, the seas grew rough and the Prince's boat could not go forward. Then his consort, Princess Oto-Tachibana, who was accompanying him, declared that she herself would go into the sea to appease the wrath of the god of the sea-crossing. She wanted the Prince to be able to carry out his mission successfully and return with his report. With that, she cast herself into the stormy waters, which immediately grew calm, and the Prince's boat was able to sail on to his appointed destination. At that time, Oto-Tachibana sang a lovely parting poem:

> Sane sashi
> Sagamu no ono ni
> Moyuru hi no
> Honaka ni tachite
> Toishi Kimi wa mo

try to get to know a foreign land, to learn before all else its ancient tales. For me, Finland is first of all the country of the Kalevala, Ireland the country of the Children of Lir and of Oisin, India the country of the Rāmāyana and the Jātaka, Mexico the country of Popul Vuh. Of course, such tales as these are not the everything of those countries, but they do make us feel familiar with other lands, and, in addition, I think they are a most enjoyable way into them.

For the past twenty or thirty years, words like 'internationalization' and 'globalization' have come to be very often heard. But might it not be said that over the past several decades—perhaps for more than a century—this had been started, though in an elementary way, in the world of children through their books? In 1996, the IBBY poster made for 'Children's Book Day' had a picture of a boy reading a book with obvious pleasure, as he lightly floated in the air above a lot of roofs that symbolized the homes of the world. In far distant places here and there around the world, for years and years already, children have been jointly reading the same tales, and have become familiar with the same storybook heroes.

In the book of ancient tales my father gave me, there was one story that I never can forget. Precise dates cannot be determined, but it is the story of a prince who lived before the 6th century. The Prince—called Yamato

Was it because I was a child myself?—I read with absorbing interest these tales of the childhood of our race. I think that the myths and legends of any one country, while they may not be accurate, factual history, symbolize the people of that country in a strange and wonderful way. When we add to this the world of folklore, we can perceive, albeit faintly, how the people of the different countries and regions responded to nature: what was their view on life and death; what they valued; what they feared.

In the sense that it taught me how, aside from our individual families, the people have a common ancestry, the book of myths and legends that my father brought gave me a something very like a root. Sometimes a book can give a child the root of stability and security. Other times it seems a book gives wings to soar and fly just anywhere. However, the root which that book gave me then was only enough to enable me to dimly perceive where I belong. Later on, it would appear to be no more than the first stage in nurturing the greater root of self-definition.

Also—and this is something I realized long afterwards—that book showed me the very prototype of the Japanese tale. It was the powerful prototype in whose spreading hems children's literature would eventually be born. And my childhood encounter with this prototype was the starting-point in me of that desire I have, when I meadow-rue, gathered and well dried for herbal use. To carry eight kilograms of dried plants by hand was too much for me. Mother tied the bundles on my back and then I carried them all the way to school. When there was no milk to be got, Mother kept a goat for my little brother, and it made me so happy that the chores of minding it and milking it were left to me.

At that time when, apart from school textbooks, there was so little reading matter to be had, what a happiness it was to get the books which Father, now and then, would bring from Tokyo! Since I had so few volumes, I would read every bit of them and I prized them highly. There was one volume among them—I do not now recall the exact title—which was a book of Japanese myths and legends for children. Telling about the early ages at the dawn of Japanese history, all these tales are found in two books written down in the 8th century, the 'Kojiki' and the 'Nihonshoki'. No doubt my book was a retelling of the tales, adapted for children.

Father is a man of few words, and I have never heard him tell, either then or later, what feelings prompted his choice of that particular book. But thinking on it now, I realize it was a truly fine gift, as the war ended shortly after that, and, under the American Army Occupation, educational policies in Japan underwent sweeping changes, so that from then on myths and legends were totally eliminated from the teaching of history.

the first hearing, I could not simply conclude 'Oh, good!' and I even had at times some vague uneasy intimations that just to go on living was no easy thing. In spite of that, I certainly did not dislike this story.

The war broke out around the time I entered elementary school. This was in 1941. About the time I was promoted to Fourth Year, the war situation deteriorated and the school-children respectively sought the help of relations or joined school groups and were evacuated to the countryside. As for my family, my father and my elder brother stayed behind in Tokyo, while I and my younger sister and brother were taken by my mother to the seaside first and then to the mountains, moving from one house to another, and we greeted the end of the war at our third evacuation home.

Such repeated moves and changing schools, and so on, are stressful for a child. Not a few memories come back to me of finding myself at something of a loss during this evacuee-life period, trying to adapt to different surroundings, different customs, and different dialects. However, I, who had been rather delicate up till then, grew strong and healthy from living in the country. I did such things as raising silkworms and cutting grass for fertilizer, and incidentally I even rose to the challenge of fulfilling the school assignment, which involved bringing in four kilograms each of leaves of wild geranium and was stuffed full with sorrows and he went off to see his friend, saying he could no longer go on living and pouring out his tale of woe. But his snail friend said, 'You are not alone in that. The shell on my back, too, is filled full of sorrows.' The little snail went to another friend and then another friend and told them the same tale of woe, but from every friend the same reply came back. So the snail at last came to realize that everyone had his burden of sorrows to bear. 'It is not only me. I, too, must bear my own burden of sorrows.' The story ends when this snail decides to stop bemoaning his lot.

What age would I have been at that time? Since Mother and Grandfather, who was Mother's father, and my uncles and aunts read to me and told me tales up to about my second year in elementary school, I think I would have been between four and seven. At that age, I had not yet known anything you could call a great sorrow. For that reason no doubt, when I learnt that in the end the little snail had stopped bemoaning his lot, I simply thought 'Oh, good!' That was all. I gave no special thought to the whole matter.

But afterwards, time and again that story kept on coming back to mind: it would seem that the sorrows that filled the shell quite full, and the sudden awareness of this, and the anxiety that made the snail feel he could no longer go on living were all indelibly engraved on my memory. As I grew a little older, unlike my response to or even after building if the bridge fails to fulfil its function, or if the will to build bridges is lost, people become helplessly isolated and lose their peace. I think, too, that our bridges must reach not only outward but inward, continuously connecting one to one's inmost self, discovering one's true self, and being an incentive to the proper setting up of the individual self.

Although I was caught up in evacuee life because of the war, the protecting hand of my elders was always there, so my childhood was a time of relative tranquillity. Nevertheless, in that situation, the repeated changes of life environment were hard to bear for a child, and I sometimes felt ill at ease with my surroundings and even was at odds with my own self, and I remember there were times when I was quite exhausted.

At such times, how much did I enjoy and how greatly was I encouraged by a few books that I had by me, which, though they could not solve each and every problem, helped me to go on! Although I fear that my limited experience may not be of much help to anyone, I shall talk about it, just as it comes back to mind.

While I was still a little girl, I was told a story of a snail. Since my memory of it is blurred, I will talk about it following the book on which it was probably based: 'The Sorrows of a Little Snail' by Niimi Nankichi. Suddenly one day, a snail became aware that the shell upon his back

'Little Blue' and 'Little Yellow', and I might never have known the history of Virginia Lee Burton's '[The] Little House'. Also, it was after I had already become a mother of children that I came to know J. R .R. Tolkien and C. S. Lewis, Rosemary Sutcliff and Philippa Pearce. But as I said earlier, I have gone through only a limited number of books, and I lack the capacity to speak from the viewpoint of the research scholar or the specialist. Again, regarding the present theme of children's literature and peace, I fear I can only make the connection between the two things in a roundabout way.

Children's literature and peace are not necessarily bound closely and directly together. Also, it goes without saying that no one book or number of books can be the key that will open wide the doors of peace. Today then, on this occasion, if there is something *I* can do, it may be to look back over my reading experiences in my own childhood and to recall a few books which left 'buds' as it were in me that burgeoned later within me into ways of thinking and of feeling; might I not try to talk about all that? Then, however little, I hope some thought can be devoted to all this in the context of 'peace', which is the theme of this Congress.

From the time they are born, people must build bridges one after another to all around them, deepening their links with other people and things, thus creating their own world to live in. If such bridges are not built, these distinguished people—their thoughts on freedom, democracy and peace—the warm welcome in which people enveloped us, the days of travel in Calcutta, New Delhi, Agra, Bombay, Bodh Gaya and Patna, all these I recall with keen nostalgia, and I pray with all my heart for the success of this IBBY Congress in India.

Regarding the theme of the Congress—Peace Through Children's Books—what kind of speech can I make? Since that day three years ago, when in March 1995 I received a letter from Mrs. Jafa, head of the Indian Branch of IBBY, I have put myself this question any number of times.

Like so many other people, up to this day I have received numerous benefits from books. In childhood I enjoyed children's books as one sphere of play. Since I grew up, I have been reading grown-up books and, although their number is not great, I continue to enjoy some children's books. After marriage, I was blessed with three children, so I had the happiness of rereading with them the children's literature I had loved as a child, as well as the joy of getting to know new works of children's literature. I consider myself very fortunate indeed.

If I had not had children, even though I knew about Little Red Ridinghood and Heidi of the Alps and the jungle where the boy Mowgli lived, I might never have encountered Marie Hall Ets' boy who played hide-and-seek with the animals deep in the forest, or Leo Lionni's

Reminiscences of
Childhood Readings

Mrs. Jafa, Mrs. Dearden, Dear Friends of IBBY

In connection with the opening of the 26th Congress of IBBY in New Delhi, I unexpectedly received an invitation to be the keynote speaker. Unfortunately, I am unable to attend the Congress in person, and it transpires that I am making my speech in this manner. From far-away Japan then, I congratulate you on the opening of this New Delhi Congress, and I thank you heartily for your kind invitation.

I have many fond memories of the Land of India, where the present Congress is being held. In 1960 I visited India, accompanying His Majesty, who was still Crown Prince then. At the time, I was twenty-six and the young mother of a nine-month-old baby. In India, which some thirteen years earlier, after long years of hope, had at last achieved independence, it was the time of President Prasad, Vice-President Radhakrishnan and Prime Minister Nehru. The days I listened with deep feeling to the conversation of

KEYNOTE SPEECH
BY
HER MAJESTY EMPRESS MICHIKO
OF JAPAN
AT
THE 26TH CONGRESS
OF THE INTERNATIONAL BOARD
ON BOOKS FOR YOUNG PEOPLE
(IBBY)
NEW DELHI (1998)

This keynote speech was delivered on videotape by Her Majesty Empress Michiko of Japan at the 26th Congress of the International Board on Books for Young People (IBBY), held at the Ashok Hotel in New Delhi from September 20th to September 24th, 1998. The speech was shortened due to limitations of time, but the parts omitted have been restored in this present edition.

BUILDING BRIDGES
reminiscences of childhood readings

Copyright © 1998 by The Empress Michiko of Japan.
All rights reserved.

English translation by Eileen Kato.
Editorial assistance by Jules Young.

Original edition published by Suemori Books Co., Ltd. 1998.
Republished by Bungeishunju Ltd. 2012.

ISBN 978-4-16-375310-2 C0095
Printed in Japan

First edition   April 2012

BUILDING BRIDGES

Reminiscences
of
Childhood
Readings

Her Majesty
Empress Michiko
of Japan

Bungeishunju

*Her Majesty in the garden of
the Imperial Palace, October 1998.*